THE SCIENCE OF NATURAL DISASTERS

THE SCIENCE OF TORNADOES

Carol Hand

Cavendish Square

Published in 2020 by Cavendish Square Publishing, LLC
243 5th Avenue, Suite 136, New York, NY 10016

Copyright © 2020 by Cavendish Square Publishing, LLC

First Edition

No part of this publication may be reproduced, stored in a retrieval system, or transmitted in any form or by any means—electronic, mechanical, photocopying, recording, or otherwise—without the prior permission of the copyright owner. Request for permission should be addressed to Permissions, Cavendish Square Publishing, 243 5th Avenue, Suite 136, New York, NY 10016. Tel (877) 980-4450; fax (877) 980-4454.

Website: cavendishsq.com

This publication represents the opinions and views of the author based on his or her personal experience, knowledge, and research. The information in this book serves as a general guide only. The author and publisher have used their best efforts in preparing this book and disclaim liability rising directly or indirectly from the use and application of this book.

All websites were available and accurate when this book was sent to press.

Library of Congress Cataloging-in-Publication Data

Names: Hand, Carol, 1945- author.
Title: The science of tornadoes / Carol Hand.
Description: First edition. | New York : Cavendish Square, [2019]. | Series: The science of natural disasters | Audience: Grades 2 to 5. | Includes bibliographical references and index.
Identifiers: LCCN 2019004950 (print) | LCCN 2019005937 (ebook) | ISBN 9781502646576 (ebook) | ISBN 9781502646569 (library bound) | ISBN 9781502646545 (pbk.) | ISBN 9781502646552 (6 pack)
Subjects: LCSH: Tornadoes--Juvenile literature. Classification: LCC QC955.2 (ebook) | LCC QC955.2 .H36245 2019 (print) | DDC 551.55/3--dc23
LC record available at https://lccn.loc.gov/2019004950

Editorial Director: David McNamara
Editor: Kristen Susienka
Copy Editor: Nathan Heidelberger
Associate Art Director: Alan Sliwinski
Designer: Ginny Kemmerer
Production Coordinator: Karol Szymczuk
Photo Research: J8 Media

The photographs in this book are used by permission and through the courtesy of: Cover Shotshop GmbH/Alamy Stock Photo, background (and used throughout the book) Lightkite/Shutterstock.com; p. 1 (and used throughout the book) Sarkelin/Shutterstock.com; p. 4 Jason Persoff/Cultura Exclusive/Getty Images; p. 6 NOAA; p. 7 Ryan McGinnis/Moment/Getty Images; p. 8 Jonathan Weiss/Shutterstock.com; p. 11, 21 Jim Reed/Corbis/Getty Images; p. 12 Dan Ross/Alamy Stock Photo; p. 14 John D. Sirlin/Shutterstock.com; p. 15 Monica Schroeder/Science Source; p. 16 Alexander Fisher/Getty Images; p. 18 NZP Chasers/Getty Images; p. 22 Tasos Katopodis/Getty Images; p. 24 Jeffrey Greenberg/UIG/Getty Images; p. 26 Milehightraveler/Getty Images; p. 28 Imagehd/Shutterstock.com.

Printed in the United States of America

CONTENTS

CHAPTER 1 What Are Tornadoes Like?..........5

CHAPTER 2 Tornado Science in Action..........13

CHAPTER 3 Planning and Preparing for a Tornado......................23

Glossary................................29

Find Out More.......................30

Index....................................31

About the Author...................32

This giant tornado touches down and roars across the landscape near Campo, Colorado.

WHAT ARE TORNADOES LIKE?

Tornadoes have the fastest winds on Earth. They destroy everything in their path. In a tornado, winds can reach speeds from 65 to 300 miles per hour (105 to 483 kilometers per hour). They travel over land at speeds between 10 and 70 miles per hour (16 to 113 kmh). Tornadoes are very scary weather events!

What Is a Tornado?

Tornadoes are also called twisters or cyclones. Their winds rotate, or turn in a circle. The rotating forms a

vortex. A vortex is a funnel-shaped whirling cloud. It is the center of a tornado. Some tornadoes have more than one vortex. Two or more are called vortices.

Some tornadoes travel less than 1 mile (1.6 kilometers) on the ground. Most travel 6 miles (9.6 km) or less. However, some travel several hundred miles. All leave a path of ruin.

Tornadoes come in many sizes. Most are about 500 to 650 feet (152 to 198 meters) across. Tiny ones are only a few feet across. The largest tornadoes can be 2 miles (3.2 km) wide.

A tornado develops from a funnel cloud and touches down near Dodge City, Kansas, in 2016.

THE SCIENCE OF TORNADOES

This house in Kokomo, Indiana, was destroyed by tornado winds in 2016.

Most tornadoes are long, thin **funnel clouds**. They start high in the air and go down to the ground. Some large tornadoes are wedge-shaped. The widest part of the wedge is in the clouds.

DID YOU KNOW?

Tornadoes occur on every continent except Antarctica. Most happen in North America. The United States has about 1,200 tornadoes every year.

WHAT ARE TORNADOES LIKE? 7

US Tornado Frequency

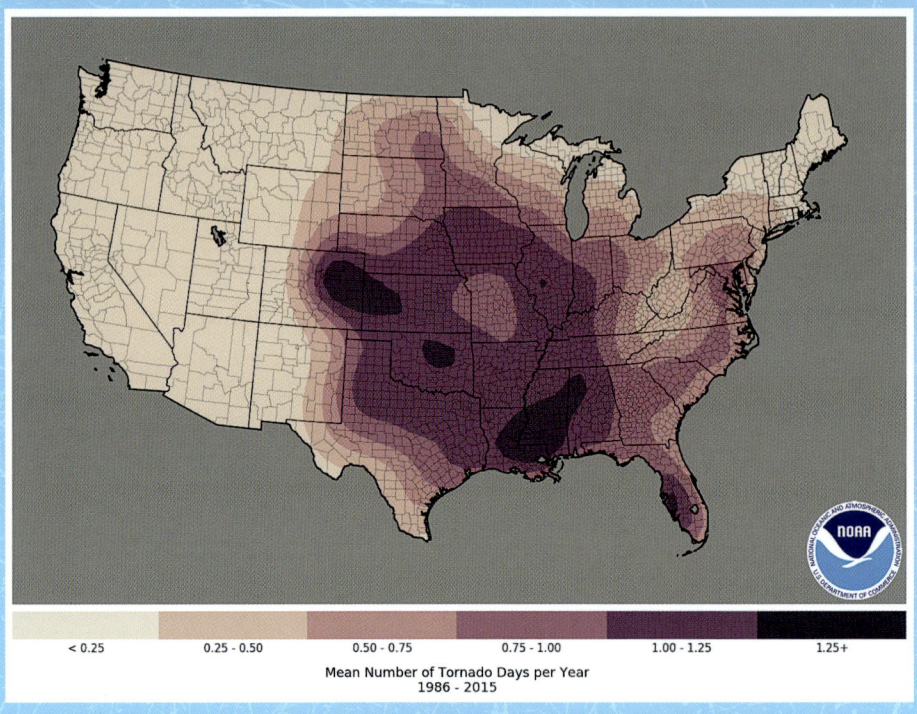

This map shows average tornado days per year between 1986 and 2015.

The darkest areas on the map above show places that had the most tornadoes between 1986 and 2015. Most tornadoes occur in the South and the Great Plains, including Texas, Oklahoma, Kansas, Nebraska, and Iowa. This area is called Tornado Alley. Florida, Louisiana, Illinois, Indiana, and Missouri also have many tornadoes.

Tornadoes can happen in any month. Most take place in April, May, and June. They can happen during any time of day or night. Most occur between 3 p.m. and 9 p.m. That is when the air is cooling. Hot air and cold air make thunderstorms.

Thunderstorms can form tornadoes. Tornadoes go in the direction of the wind. They usually move from southwest to northeast.

These tornado chasers gather data on a supercell thunderstorm that unfolds in the distance.

Spotting a Tornado

There are several warning signs that a tornado is coming. The sky turns very dark and greenish. There is

DID YOU KNOW?

Tornadoes develop very fast and are hard to study. People who study tornadoes sometimes go to get a better view. They are called tornado chasers. They study tornadoes up close using special equipment.

often large hail. Before a tornado, the wind usually dies down. The air becomes very still. A funnel cloud forms high in the sky. When a tornado is close, it makes a roaring sound, like a train.

Tornadoes often come from the bottom of a **wall cloud**. Wall clouds are wide clouds below thunderstorm clouds. They are sometimes up to 2 miles (3.2 km) wide. They are areas with no rain but with a strong **updraft**. Air gets sucked up into the wall cloud and begins to rotate.

Tornadoes are very dangerous. They can move very fast and change direction. People can be hurt or killed by the flying trash in tornado winds. The average time to warn people about a tornado is only fifteen minutes. It is important to stay far from tornadoes.

A massive wedge-shaped tornado crosses Illinois farmland in 2015.

TORNADO SCIENCE IN ACTION

Tornadoes form from thunderstorms. They need several things to form. These include **moisture**, unstable air, and heat energy. The air needs to be warm, so most tornadoes happen in the spring or summer. Tornadoes only form when weather conditions are just right.

Building a Tornado

Tornadoes happen during or after thunderstorms. They are "built" by different parts of the atmosphere. Warm, moist air near the ground rises and cools. Lots of water vapor, or gas, in the air gathers to form rain clouds. As water vapor changes to rain, it releases heat energy. The heat energy powers the thunderstorm.

If there is enough energy, the rising air begins to whirl. This can become a tornado. The storm gets stronger in unstable air. Air is unstable if its temperature and moisture are very different from top to bottom. Other ingredients needed to form a tornado are: **wind shear**, updraft, a storm, and a supercell.

Thunderstorms release electrical energy as lightning.

Wind shear occurs when winds act differently at different heights in the atmosphere. If they blow at different speeds depending

14   THE SCIENCE OF TORNADOES

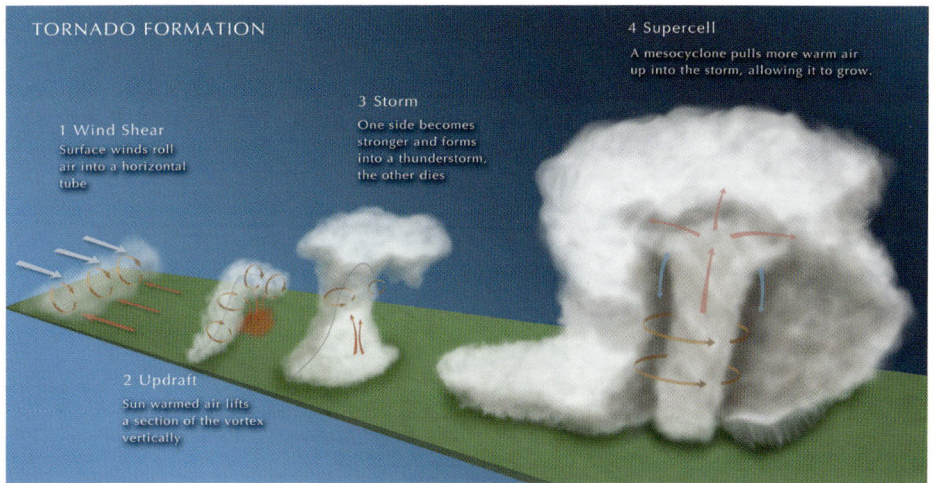

This illustration shows the stages tornadoes need to form: wind shear, updraft, storm, and supercell.

on their height, it's called speed shear. If they blow in different directions, it's called directional sheer. Speed shear determines how fast a tornado will move, and directional shear determines how fast the tornado spins. For tornadoes to form in the first place, directional shear is needed. Slower-moving air on the ground rises and changes direction. It also gets faster. As the air starts to spin, a tornado can form.

A tornado also needs updraft to form. Updraft is an upward movement of air. It happens when warm, moist

Rotation is visible in this giant updraft seen in Colorado.

air moves up from the ground. All storms have updrafts. Updrafts are usually vertical. However, when speed shear increases, an updraft tilts. This means a storm can make a tornado that lasts for a long time.

The third stage is the storm itself. The updraft sucks in air from the ground. It creates two or more vertical vortices. The largest one continues to grow and becomes a thunderstorm. The thunderstorm can build into a larger storm, called a supercell storm.

A supercell storm is a very large thunderstorm with rotating winds. If all the other ingredients are present, the supercell storm becomes a tornado.

Inside a Tornado

We know the winds around the outside of a tornado whirl rapidly. But what happens inside? Most people who get close enough to see inside a tornado do not live. But in the 1920s and 1950s, two farmers did. They survived because the tornadoes did not quite touch the ground as they passed over them.

DID YOU KNOW?

Most supercells form thunderstorms. Three out of ten form tornadoes. No one is sure why only some supercells form tornadoes. Most tornadoes die because colder air or rain changes the flow of air spinning the tornado.

A supercell has a deep rotating updraft called a mesocyclone (seen here). This giant supercell has formed a tornado (*right*).

Will Keller lived in Kansas. His experience occurred in 1928. Roy Hall was from Texas. His story happened in 1951. Both said that inside the tornado it was very still. The center was clear and circular. The rotating walls were smooth. Lightning streaked across the walls. It made a bluish light. Keller also talked about a strong gas smell. Both described tinier tornadoes forming on the tornado walls and breaking free.

HOW DO YOU RATE THAT?

The Enhanced Fujita Scale (EF Scale) rates tornadoes. The scale is named for T. Theodore Fujita. Fujita was a **meteorologist**. He designed the scale. The EF Scale tells the wind speed of a tornado. It describes the kind of damage it causes. Higher numbers mean more damage and faster wind speed.

EF0:	65–85 mph (105–137 kmh)	Light damage
EF1:	86–110 mph (138–177 kmh)	Moderate damage
EF2:	111–135 mph (178–217 kmh)	Considerable damage
EF3:	136–165 mph (218–266 kmh)	Severe damage
EF4:	166–200 mph (267–322 kmh)	Devastating damage
EF5:	over 200 mph (over 322 kmh)	Incredible damage

DID YOU KNOW?

According to the Storm Prediction Center, about 8 percent of tornadoes occur in winter, 43 percent in spring, 35 percent in summer, and 15 percent in fall.

Other Tornadoes

Not all tornadoes come from supercell storms. Some form in air near the ground. Wind shear occurs, with air of different temperatures coming together. This causes the air to spin. If spinning air moves along the ground and an updraft moves over it, the air is stretched. A tornado forms. These tornadoes are usually small.

Three types of non-supercell tornadoes are gustnadoes, landspouts, and waterspouts. A gustnado is a whirling mass of dust or litter near the ground. It does not have a funnel cloud. It forms along the front of a storm. A landspout is narrow and rope-like. Its funnel cloud forms in front of a thunderstorm. There is no rotating updraft, so the spinning motion begins near the ground. A waterspout is like a landspout, but it forms over water.

This landspout tornado occurred in western Kansas.

DID YOU KNOW?

A tornado watch means a tornado might happen. A tornado warning means a tornado has been seen. If you see an alert for a tornado warning, you should find shelter immediately.

TORNADO SCIENCE IN ACTION

An EF4 tornado caused this path of destruction across Washington, Illinois, in November 2013.

CHAPTER 3

PLANNING AND PREPARING FOR A TORNADO

People must be prepared before a tornado happens. They should make a plan in advance. This helps them know what to do if a tornado occurs.

Plan and Prepare

Your family should have a safe place to go during a tornado. The best place is the lowest level of your house or building. This might be a basement or ground-floor room. It's important that the room does not have windows. Family pets should stay with you.

You should listen to weather forecasts on local radio stations. You should know what to do if a tornado warning is posted. If your state gets a lot of tornadoes, cities will often sound sirens to alert people. You should take cover if bad weather is around and you hear the siren.

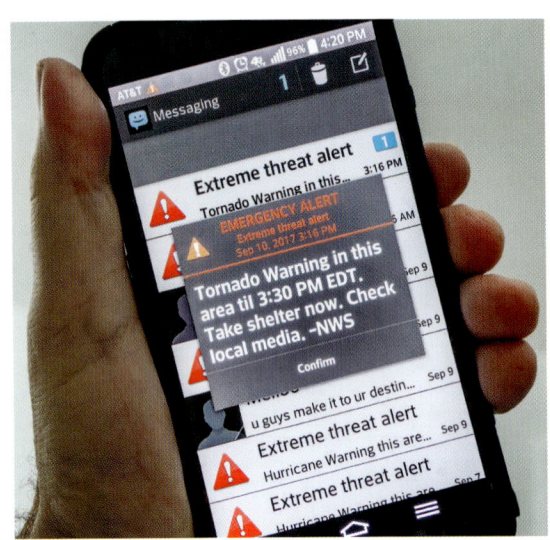

Smartphones give up-to-date tornado warnings.

Your family should have an emergency kit. The kit should have a flashlight, a battery-operated radio and extra batteries, medicines, a first-aid kit, and food and water for each family member (including pets) for three

24 **THE SCIENCE OF TORNADOES**

DID YOU KNOW?

Southern Canada gets about one hundred known tornadoes every year. Most of these are in Saskatchewan, Alberta, and Ontario. Most Canadian tornadoes occur in July.

days. Choose food that doesn't need to be cooked to be eaten. Don't forget a can opener!

During and After a Tornado

The safest place during a tornado is indoors and low to the ground. If you can get inside, cover your head with a pillow or a mattress. Covering up prevents being injured by flying objects. If you are outside, look for an open area. Do not hide under trees and overpasses. Lie flat in a ditch.

TORNADO TECH: DOPPLER RADAR

Doppler radar helps people understand storms.

Doppler radar helps forecast tornadoes. Radar sends out radio waves that hit **particles** in the air. After they hit, the radio waves return to a satellite system. The satellites take in information and send it to meteorologists. Using data from radar, meteorologists determine a storm's speed and direction. This helps them predict when or if a tornado will happen.

Today, scientists want to make Doppler radar better. They want it to be possible to tell whether a particle is rain or hail. They also want to send out several radar beams at once to see storm changes faster. People are working on these improvements, but they are not quite ready to use.

After a tornado, dangerous electrical wires or sharp objects might be on the ground. Do not enter an area until a rescue worker says it is safe. If you are trapped, do not move large objects. This may cause a collapse. Instead, tap on the object trapping you. This will tell rescuers where you are.

Tornadoes are hard to predict. This tornado happened in Canada.

Forecasting Tornadoes

Earth's climate is changing. Today, there are more storms, and they are getting stronger. We need better forecasting methods. But tornadoes are hard to predict. Meteorologists use four technologies to predict tornadoes: weather balloons, satellites, radar,

Weather balloons help scientists track storm and weather conditions.

and weather-station data. They also look at temperature and wind data over time. Data on moisture, wind shear, and temperature differences help them predict how likely storms are.

Forecasters are working to increase the warning time to longer than fifteen minutes. They also want to link weather stations across the country so they can receive data more quickly.

Tornadoes can be deadly, wherever they happen. However, better prediction and better technology can keep people safe.

GLOSSARY

funnel cloud A fast-rotating cloud in the sky that forms a tornado.

meteorologist A scientist who studies weather.

moisture Wet air.

particles Small elements in a cloud, like hail, rain, or snow.

updraft A current of warm, moist air moving upward from the ground.

vortex A whirling or rotating wind, like that found in a tornado.

wall cloud A very broad cloud at the base of a thunderstorm; an area with no rain but strong updraft.

wind shear A difference in wind speed or direction at different heights.

FIND OUT MORE

Books

Simon, Seymour. *Tornadoes*. New York: HarperCollins Publishers, 2017.

Wendorff, Anne. *Tornadoes*. Blastoff! Readers: Extreme Weather. Minneapolis, MN: Bellwether Media, 2016.

Website

Weather WizKids: Tornadoes

http://www.weatherwizkids.com/weather-tornado.htm

This site gives short answers to questions about tornadoes.

Video

How Do Tornadoes Form?

https://www.youtube.com/watch?v=xSEXoy46_vA

This brief video describes tornado formation as a rap.

INDEX

Page numbers in **boldface** refer to images. Entries in **boldface** are glossary terms.

alerts, 21, 24, **24**
damage, 5, **7**, 11, 19, **22**, 27
EF Scale, 19, **19**
formation, 11, 13–17, **15**, 20–21
funnel cloud, 4, 6–7, **6**, 11, **12**, 21, **27**
heat energy, 13–16, **15**
inside a tornado, 17–18
landspout, 20–21, **21**
meteorologist, 19, 26–28

moisture, 13–16, 28
particles, 26
predicting, 26–28
safety, 23–25, 27
supercell, **10**, 14, **15**, 16–17, **18**, 20
thunderstorms, 9, 11, 13–14, **14**, **15**, 16–17, 21
updraft, 11, 14–16, **15**, 20–21
vortex, 5–6, 16
wall cloud, 11
warning signs, 10–11
where/when tornadoes occur, 7–9, **8**, 20, 25
wind shear, 14–16, **15**, 20, 28

INDEX 31

ABOUT THE AUTHOR

Carol Hand is a science writer specializing in earth and life sciences. Hand has a PhD in zoology and previously worked as a college teacher and curriculum specialist. She has written more than fifty science and technology books for young people, including titles on glaciers, weather patterns, and climate change. One of her books describes another natural disaster, avalanches.